# TATOES YOU LIKE

## MEENA MISTRY

Balboa Press books may be ordered through booksellers or by contacting:

Balboa Press
A Division of Hay House
1663 Liberty Drive
Bloomington, IN 47403
www.balboapress.com
844-682-1282

Because of the dynamic nature of the Internet, any web addresses or links contained in this book may have changed since publication and may no longer be valid. The views expressed in this work are solely those of the author and do not necessarily reflect the views of the publisher, and the publisher hereby disclaims any responsibility for them.

ISBN: 979-8-7652-3942-1 (sc)
ISBN: 979-8-7652-3943-8 (e)

Library of Congress Control Number: 2023903193

Print information available on the last page.

Balboa Press rev. date:    05/30/2023

BALBOA.PRESS
A DIVISION OF HAY HOUSE

# Contents

# Dedications

This book is dedicated to my special daughters Kunjal and Neera and grandson Ivan. Their enthusiasm, inspiration, and support have given me an opportunity to dwell in the world of potatoes and come up with unique recipes and associated meals full taste and culinary diversity.

# Acknowledgements

A potato is an amazing vegetable which has been around for many years in different forms and contributes significantly in the kitchen from dietary and complementary perspectives. The basic potato can easily be infused with other ingredients and worked upon to potentially result in a variety of foods that cover multiple cultures around the world.

The love and passion of creating recipes and cooking runs in my blood and goes back many years ago to the region of Kilimanjaro, Tanzania where I was born and, in the U.K., where I lived for many years. This joy of cooking evolved further and dramatically over the many years through effective use of spices and herbs for diversified vegetarian cooking which continued when I relocated to the United States in 2006.

The experiences of getting my books "Spicy N Easy" and "Vege Kick" published in 2013 and in 2020 respectively gave me further opportunities to cultivate culinary skills for vegetarian cooking through unique and careful selection and combination of spices, herbs and a variety of vegetables. Mistry successfully continues to use multiple ingredients for creating tasty fusion vegetarian meals through her influential British upbringing and skills with minimal effort for every household member to enjoy.

"TATOES YOU LIKE" takes us into an amazing journey of a potato, its brief history, its versatility as a food ingredient, its benefits from a dietary perspective and its ability to be modified for its taste and texture as a food item for consumption.

Through my influential British upbringing and culinary skills my aim is to demonstrate the versatility of vegetarian ingredients in creating unique recipes using the basic but very the important potato. You will find this book fascinating to read and practical to have it in a kitchen to prepare a home meal full of flavor and taste. I would like to thank my friends, daughters and husband Anuj for their continued support. Thank you.

**Meena Mistry**

# Introduction

Vegetarian cooking is an art that requires skill and perfection. Individuals choosing to follow a vegetarian diet often choose additional healthy lifestyle habits such as regular physical exercise, frequent exposure to sunlight and fresh air. A healthy vegetarian diet is one in which a variety and abundance of plant-based foods such as grains, legumes, vegetables, herbs and spices are primarily eaten.

All lentils and pulses are nutritious and play an important part in vegetarian diet. They are excellent sources of fibre and protein and are low in cholesterol and fat. I have included a few recipes based on these in this book for a balanced approach to being a vegetarian.

Herbs and spices continue to play an integral role in cooking for taste, flavors and quite often are complementary for multiple health reasons.

Spices result from seeds, roots, berries and certain stems and usually native to warm tropical climates. These are dried and used in powder or ground form or whole. It is the volatile oils in the herbs and spices that provide some of the useful properties namely flavoring, aroma, preservation and medicinal that are beneficial in culinary.

The secret of a successful and a tasty recipe is significantly contributed by such ingredients. While they give a flavour and aroma to the food being cooked it is the right combination of them which makes the overall contribution to the recipe. Spices and herbs not only give that desired taste to the food, they also provide positive medicinal effects on the body.

It will be interesting to review key spices and herbs of which some have been used in the recipes. They go a long way to give the flavor and aroma for one to enjoy a meal.

Coriander is used as an add-on spice to enhance flavoring and is commonly found both as whole dried seeds and in powder form. Seeds may be heated on a dry pan briefly before grinding to enhance and alter the aroma. The seeds are shaped as tiny balls and they give that distinctive spicy sweet flavor. They are used as a flavoring for food and as a seasoning as well as in curries and curry powder.

Cilantro is essentially coriander leaves which have a sage-citrus flavor and an almost pungent aroma. Chopped cilantro is used for seasoning and garnishing and is very popular in Latin American and Asian foods. It is always best to use fresh cilantro when using for culinary seasoning since its aroma is optimized.

Cumin is a dried seed of the parsley family. Cumin is used as a spice for its distinctive peppery aroma and is very popular in India and Asian cuisines. This is an essential ingredient for preparing vegetarian curries and many appetizers in whole or ground form.

Chilies are used fresh green or red and in powder form for most preparations to provide a unique flavor and hotness in the food. Quite often one wants to have the chili flavor but without that hotness. In this case one can remove the seeds from the whole chili and add the rest becomes part of the ingredients in finely chopped form. It is wise to use chilies sparingly during cooking. Sometimes may decide to put chili powder in ready cooked food to give additional hotness.

Cinnamon is primarily used as a condiment and provides a distinct pungent sweet flavoring. Cinnamon grows as brown bark which upon drying, rolls into a tubular form. Cinnamon can be bought either its whole form (sticks) or as ground powder. Cinnamon sticks are quite often used in preparing rice dishes and various dal soups.

Cloves are dried buds of the clove tree. Cloves are used as a spice in cuisines all over the world to give that unique almost bitter sweet flavor. They can be used in cooking either whole or in a ground form. Use cloves in small amounts since they are extremely are used sparingly.

Garlic has a characteristic pungent, spicy flavor that mellows extremely well with cooking as a condiment. Its intense aroma and health benefits certainly make a mark in the food it is used in.

Ginger is a rhizome tuber that is frequently used to provide a peppery sweet flavor and preservative capabilities. For best results and effectiveness, it is very wise to use freshly grated ginger when preparing foods. It provides excellent aroma and taste when used for a number of dishes such lentils, pulses and tikka varieties.

Mustard seeds have a special place in culinary and is often used for garnishing during which the seeds are quickly and lightly fried in oil as a prerequisite for curry and similar and similar dish preparations. Mustard seeds provide a pungent, nutty but a nutritious flavoring.

Turmeric is part of the ginger family that has found itself uniquely in Asian and Persian cuisines for its taste, reported medicinal and coloring ability. It gives a warm and aromatic flavor when used in correct amount.

The health benefits of herbs and spices are widely known and reported. I have been very fortunate to be in a position to witness and experience most of these benefits and to be able to associate these with creation of my recipes. Spices can be useful and be beneficial if used correctly and in right proportions.

Cilantro and cumin are known to assist in digestion, flatulence and upset stomach. They are also sources of iron and magnesium.

Cumin aids in digestion, common cold, anemia, skin disorders additionally boost our immune system.

Chilies, in moderation, contribute significantly when it comes to aiding health. They are known to prevent sinusitis and help remove mucus from your nose and relieve congestion. Additionally chilies help combat inflammation and soothe intestinal diseases. Chilies are potentially thermogenic and they assist in fat metabolism resulting in increased body heat.

Cinnamon equally is beneficial to our dietary habits. Various benefits of cinnamon have been reported. These include lowering of cholesterol, regulate blood sugar, anti-clotting effecting on blood and acts like a natural food preservative and is a good source of fiber, manganese, calcium and iron.

Clove and clove oil have successfully been used for toothaches, respiratory problems, and indigestion and as an antiseptic. Clove oil is also known to assist with blood circulation and purification. Cloves contain manganese, omega 3 fatty acids, vitamins K and C and fiber and are a good all round health supplement.

The potential benefits of Garlic are reportedly more pronounced and effective when eaten freshly chopped or crushed and in moderation. Garlic has been known to help with cardiovascular and high cholesterol conditions.

Ginger appears to help fight morning sickness, reduce pain and inflammation. It is also reported to help relieve heart burn, motion sickness, cold and flu.

Mustard is one of the most popular spices and contributes significantly as a beneficial source of nutritional health. It contains omega 3 fatty acids, iron, fiber and other minerals. It has the ability to be stimulating digestion.

Turmeric is probably one of the most powerful spices which has found its use in many cultures. The inherent health benefits of turmeric have gradually surfaced over hundreds of years. It has successfully been used in Asia for its anti-inflammatory properties, wound healing, skin disorders and many more.

The idea to review the benefits is to bring an awareness and realization of how these benefits can be successfully incorporated in cooking, especially in vegetarian cooking.

Being vegetarian has its potential proven benefits but to compliment vegetables and ingredients classed as vegetarian with spices and herbs that were discussed earlier, takes a relatively new prospective as part of healthy life style. These vegetables can be green and leafy or simply in a form of a starchy tuber. I would like to dwell further in the latter and focus on the potato in this book.

A potato finds itself uniquely embedded in many cultures as a staple food and in many countries. History of the potato goes back to Peru and Bolivia circa 7000 BCE and roughly 10,000 years in South America. It is amazing that the potato tuber has since then spread around the world. While having a nutritional value for a balanced meal, a potato can be cooked in many different ways for a satisfactory meal.

A potato is a classed as a starchy vegetable and has multiple benefits. It is a source of carbohydrates which in turn breakdowns into glucose for energy. Additionally, it is a good source of fiber, potassium, vitamin C, antioxidants and minerals all of which play a significant role in our bodily functions and it is good to know that potatoes are also gluten free in their raw form. There are multiple types of potatoes that can be seen and end up in a kitchen. Most common ones that are being bought are russet potatoes, red potatoes, white potatoes, purple potatoes, sweet potatoes and fingerling potatoes. In essence a potato has found itself in a unique spot for nutritional requirements as well as for multiple recipes in the kitchen. Potatoes can be eaten in many forms for example baked potatoes, mashed potatoes, chips and fries. These are well known across the culinary world however, my goal is to diversify the use of the potatoes and turn them into unique recipes for everyone to enjoy so let us do it.

# Potato Swirls

# Ingredients

2 large potatoes cut in wedges
¼ cup cooking oil
2 tbsp curry powder
Salt to taste
1 tbsp crushed garlic
1 packet of short crust pastry

# Procedure

1. In a bowl add potato wedges, cooking oil, curry powder, salt and crushed garlic.
2. Mix well and cook in microwave for 15 minutes and let it cool down.
3. Cut short crust pastry in strips of half inch wide.
4. Roll the pastry strips over the potato wedges.
5. Bake in pre-heated oven at 380F for 15-20 minutes or until golden brown.

**Serves: 2-4**

# Savory Vege Bakes

## Ingredients

2 cups rice flour
½ cup chick pea flour
2 cups mix vegetables
2 cups grated potatoes
2 tsp baking powder
2 cups water
3 tsp salt
2 tsp sugar
¼ cup lemon juice
¼ cup sesame seeds

## Procedure

1. In a bowl add all ingredients and mix well.
2. Drop them in a medium size muffin tray with scoop and sprinkle sesame seeds.
3. Bake in a pre-heated oven at 380F for 30- 40 minutes until dark golden brown.

**Makes 18**

# Potato and Feta Flat Bread

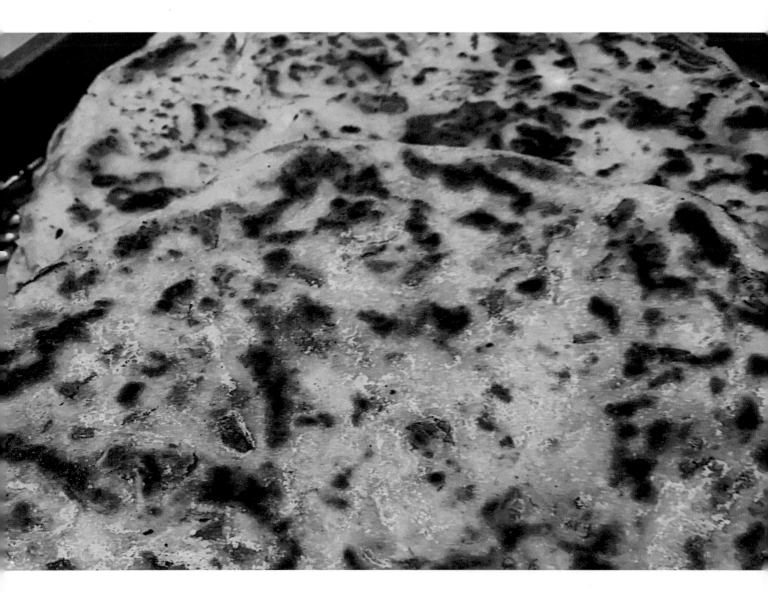

# Ingredients (Stuffing)

2 cups boiled and shredded potatoes
¾ cup feta cheese
¾ cup chopped onions
2 tbsp chopped hot chilies (optional)
¼ tsp salt
2 tbsp fresh lemon juice

In a bowl mix all stuffing ingredients well with a spoon and make 8 equal portions and flatten them into 3-inch diameter patties.

# Ingredients (Flat Bread)

2 cups brown flour
2 cups finely chopped spinach
2 tsp dried yeast
1/4 tsp salt
2 ¼ cups water

## Procedure

1. Bind all bread ingredients in a bowl and leave it aside for raise; makes 8 flat doughs
2. Roll them using a rolling pin into about 8 inches diameter circles
3. Place one patty on the flat rolled circles.
4. Fold the edges over the patty all the way round and sprinkle flour on top.
5. Flatten the stuffed circles with a rolling pin into 6-inch circles.
6. Brush each side with oil and shallow fry on a flat pan turning occasionally and until golden brown

## Serves 4-6

# Purple Potato Squeak

## Ingredients

2 cups boiled white potatoes and mashed
2 tbs butter
½ cup milk
½ cup grated cheese
5-6 purple baby potatoes boiled, peeled and cut in half.
¾ cup grated cheddar cheese to sprinkle on the top

## Procedure

1. In a bowl add mashed white potatoes, butter, milk and ½ cup cheese and mix well.
2. Spread the mashed mixture in a baking tray.
3. Evenly stick the purple potatoes over it and sprinkle the ¾ grated cheese.
4. Bake in a pre-heated oven at 380F for 15-20 mins or until golden brown.

**Serves 2**

# Chinese Style Potato Parcels

## Ingredients (Soya sauce for parcel)

2 tbsp oil
6 tbsp garlic paste
1-1 ½ cup soya sauce
1 cup water and 1 tsp corn starch mixed well together
2 chopped spring onions

1. Add all the ingredients in a pan and cook until it thickens; add spring onions last.

## Ingredients (potatoes)

12-15 boiled and peeled potatoes
12-15 spring roll sheets
Oil for brushing sheets

1. Place one sheet and put 1 tbsp of soya sauce and a potato in one corner and roll like spring roll.
2. Take another sheet and brush the edges with oil; place pre-rolled potato in the center, take 4 corners and twist the top.
3. Bake in pre-heated oven on 380F for 15- 20 mins or until crispy golden brown

**Makes 12-15**

# Potato Fritters

# Ingredients

2 large potatoes
½ cup corn flour
½ cup gram flour
¼ tsp turmeric powder
2 tsp sugar or sweetener
2 tbsp lemon juice
½ cup cilantro
Salt to taste
¼ to ½ cup water
Oil for deep frying

# Procedure

1. Peel potatoes and make about 2 mm thick slices
2. In a bowl, add all ingredients and mix well
3. Fry slices of the battered potatoes until golden brown.
4. Serve with a dip of your choice.

**Serves: 4-6**

# Rosemary Parmesan Potatoes

# Ingredients

4 cups boiled and mashed potato
½ cup Parmesan
1 ½ cup onion
4 tbsp chopped rosemary
1 tbsp finely chopped chilies (optional)
2 tbsp lemon
3 ½ tsp salt
2 tsp sugar

# Procedure

1. Mix everything in bowl
2. Make round balls

# Batter

2 cups all-purpose flour
2 tbsp cornstarch
1 ½ tsp salt
½ tsp baking soda
2 cups water
Oil for deep frying

1. Mix all batter ingredients in a bowl.
2. Dip each of the balls in batter with a spoon and fry them until golden brown, turning occasionally.

**Serves:4-6**

# Flat Potato in Bread Crumbs

## Ingredients (Gluten Free for batter)

1 cup quinoa flour
½ cup buckwheat flour
1 ½ tsp salt
½ tsp chili powder
1 tsp baking powder
2 tbsp corn starch
1 ¾ cup water
2 large boiled and peeled potatoes
Garlic paste
2 cups breadcrumbs

## Procedure

1. Slice potatoes ¼ inch thick and make a sandwich using garlic paste.
2. Add all batter ingredients in a bowl and mix well.
3. Take each potato sandwich and dip in batter followed by applying bread crumbs.
4. Deep fry until golden brown.

**Serves: 4**

# Purple Potato, Spinach and Onion Mix

## Ingredients

¼ cup oil
1 finely chopped garlic
1 small purple onion sliced
2 cups boiled purple potatoes
2 cups spinach
¼ tsp chili powder
Salt to taste

## Procedure

1. In a pan, add oil, garlic, onions and toss for 3 minutes.
2. Add rest of the ingredients and cook for 5 minutes

**Serves: 2**

# Potato, Onion and Cheese Pie

# Ingredients

6 baby potatoes boiled & peeled
1 cup chopped onion
3 tbsp olive oil
¼ tsp salt
¼ tsp black pepper
2 tsp white flour
1 ½ cup water
½ cup grated goats' cheese OR grated cheddar cheese
Puff pastry

# Procedure

1. In a pan add oil and onions, fry for two minutes.
2. Add white flour and mix well; add milk and cook until the mixture thickens to make sauce.
3. Cut potatoes in half and add to the sauce.
4. Use two 4-inch pie dishes.
5. Roll puff pastry into 5-inch diameter and 2 mm thickness circles; make four of these.
6. Lay one circle on base of each pie dish and pour mixture equally and sprinkle cheese.
7. Cover these with the remaining two circles pressing the edges to seal.
8. Bake in pre-heated oven at 380 F for 40-45 mins or until golden brown.

**Serves: 2**

# Masala Potatoes and Veges

# Ingredients

3 cups boiled small potatoes
1 cupped chopped pepper
2 onions
4 large mushrooms
¼ cup olive oil
¼ cup butter chicken powder
½ tsp salt
½ tsp chili powder
½ tsp turmeric powder

# Procedure

1. In bowl toss all ingredients together.
2. Skewer them equally and bake for 15-20 minutes turning once.
3. May be eaten with rice or couscous.

**Serves 4**

# Potato Cups with Goats Cheese

## Ingredients

5 partially boiled medium size peeled potatoes
1 cup milk
2 tbsp butter
2/3 cup water
¼ cup all-purpose flour
Salt to taste
1½ cups crumbled goat's cheese
2 strips chopped spring onions

## Procedure

1. Cut potatoes in half and core 1/3 deep down; leave aside.
2. For white sauce, add milk and butter in a pan bring to boil.
3. Mix water and flour in a small jug and mix well. Add this mixture to the boiled milk slowly while stirring and add half cup cheese mixing well to the make the sauce.
4. Fill each potato with the sauce and sprinkle rest of the cheese over them.
5. Bake in pre-heated oven at 380F for 30-40 minutes.
6. Garnish with spring onions.

**Serves 4**

# Vege Cottage Pie

# Ingredients

2 tbsp cooking oil
3 strips Rosemary
3 chopped carrots
1 large chopped potato
1 chopped leek
½ tsp cumin powder
1 red onion
2 cloves crushed garlic
3 tbsp tomato puree
½ tsp chili powder
2 tbsp lemon juice
600 ml hot water
2 lbs. potatoes boiled & mashed with butter and milk
8in. X 8in. baking tray

# Procedure

1. In a pan add oil rosemary, carrots, leek, potatoes and cook for 5 minutes; then add cumin, onion, garlic, tomato puree, chili powder, lemon juice and cook for further 10 minutes.
2. Put above cooked ingredients in the tray and cover evenly with mash potatoes.
3. Bake in pre-heated oven at 380F for 40-50 minutes.

**Serves 4-6**

# Parmesan Potatoes

## Ingredients

4 cups boiled and peeled baby potatoes
2 tbsp parmesan & pizza seasoning
½ tsp salt
Dash of chili flakes

## Procedure

1. Mix all ingredients in a pan and heat for 5-7 minutes (can be microwaved as well).
2. Can be eaten hot or cold.

**Serves 4**

# Cheesy Pasta and Potato Croquettes

## Ingredients

1 cup boiled ziti pasta
½ tsp salt
½ tsp black pepper
2 tbsp butter
2 tbsp white flour
½ cup water
¼ cup powdered parmesan
3 cups boiled mash potatoes

## Batter

1 cup all-purpose flour
¼ tsp baking powder
½ tsp salt
1½ cup water
1 ½ cups of panko bread crumbs

## Procedure

1. In a pan add butter, flour, salt, pepper and water; cook (3 minutes) until it all binds together.
2. Add pasta, and mix and let it cool down.
3. Make six equal round balls.
4. Divide the mashed potatoes into six equal parts.
5. Cover each pasta ball with mash potato to make the croquet and freeze overnight.
6. For batter mix flour, baking powder, salt, water and mix well.
7. Dip each croquet in batter followed in bread crumbs and deep fry thoroughly on medium heat until golden brown

# Spicy Buttery Potatoes in a Bun

# Ingredients

¼ cup oil
4 tbs curry masala
1 cup tin tomato sauce
3 tbs tomato paste
1 medium size onion
2 cloves garlic
½ tsp turmeric powder
½ tsp coriander powder
¼ tsp cardamom powder
2 tsp sugar
2 tsp salt
1 tsp chili powder
½ cup fresh cream
3 cups of boiled and peeled baby potatoes

# Procedure

1. In a pan mix all ingredients and cook for 7-10 minutes.
2. Can be eaten with bread roll.

**Serves 4**

# Potato with Baby Corn

# Ingredients

4 cups boiled baby potatoes
1 cup baby corn
1 cup chopped green peppers
¼ cup oil
2 tsp crushed garlic
½ cup dark soya sauce
1 tsp corn starch
2 tbsp siracha sauce
Salt to taste
2 strings of chopped spring onions

# Procedure

1. In a pan, add all ingredients (except green onions) and cook for 10 minutes, stirring occasionally.
2. Sprinkle onions for garnishing just before serving.

**Serves 4**

# Potato and Pesto Gratin

# Ingredients

1 cup crumbles crackers
1 tsp butter
½ tsp cream cheese
1 ½ tbsp pesto
½ cup grated cheese
1 cup sliced boiled potato
Two 4-inch baking trays with loose bottom

# Procedure

1. In a bowl, add crumbled crackers, butter and cream cheese; microwave for 1 minute.
2. Divide the crumbled mix into two equal parts and place them into the baking trays and pressed down with a spoon.
3. Mix potatoes and pesto in a bowl.
4. Form layers of potatoes and cheese in the trays.
5. Bake in pre-heated oven at 380 F for 30-35 minutes.

**Makes 2**

# Cheesy Potato Basket

## Ingredients for bread

1 ½ cup all-purpose flour
1 tbsp yeast
½ tsp sugar
½ tsp salt
1 tbsp olive oil
¾ cup warm water
8-inch round baking tray

## Filling

20 boiled and peeled baby potatoes
¼ cup butter
1 tsp oregano
½ tsp salt
1½ cups grated cheese
10-inch plate for serving

## Procedure

1. In a bowl add all ingredients of bread to bin; leave aside for 10-15 minutes for raise.
2. In a baking tray spread ½ cup of cheese and lay all the potatoes.
3. Sprinkle oregano, salt and place chunks of butter evenly and spread rest of the cheese.
4. Make an 8 ½ inch circle of the raised dough, cover the potatoes while tucking the edges.
5. Leave aside 20 minutes to raise and bake in a pre-heated oven at 380F for 30-35 minutes.
6. Place serving plate on top of the baking tray and flip over to release the cheesy potato basket.

# Potato Lasagna Rolls

# Ingredients

6 boiled lasagna sheets
2 cups milk
4 tbsp butter
1tsp Dijon mustard
¼ tsp nutmeg powder
2 cups water
1/3 cup all-purpose flour, Salt to taste
2 cups grated mozzarella cheese
6 boiled baby potatoes
¼ cup chopped parsley
8in.X 8in. baking tray

# Procedure

1. For white sauce, add milk and butter in a pan bring to boil.
2. Mix water and flour in a small jug and mix well. Add this mixture to the boiled milk slowly while stirring and add 1 cup cheese mixing well to the make the sauce.
3. Place a lasagna sheet flat and paste white sauce with a spoon. Repeat for remaining sheets.
4. Place 1 potato at the end of the lasagna sheet and roll; repeat for the remaining sheets.
5. In a baking tray, place rolled up sheet upright; pour remaining white sauce equally.
6. Sprinkle remaining cheese and parsley equally.
7. Bake in pre-heated oven at 380F for 30-40 minutes.

**Serves 3-4**

# Potato and Vegetable Cheese Rolls

# Ingredients

3 cups all-purpose flour
1 ½ tsp fast raising yeast
2 tbs olive oil
1 tsp salt
1 tsp sugar
1 ¼ cups water
2 cups peeled and diced potatoes
1 cup chopped green peppers
2 cups chopped onions
1 ½ cups grated cheese of your choice

# Procedure (for bread rolls)

1. In a bowl, add all ingredients and bind into dough.
2. Divide dough into two equal parts and leave side for 20 minutes.
3. Put the potatoes, peppers, onions and cheese in a bowl and mix with a spoon.
4. Roll each dough approx. 8 inches diameter.
5. Spread the mixed vegetables equally onto the two rolled doughs.
6. Fold each of them into a square parcel and leave aside for a rise for 20 minutes.
7. Bake at 380 F for about 20 minutes.

**Serves 2**

# Potatoes Stuffed in Sweet Peppers

## Ingredients

2 tbsp oil
1 cup mashed potato
Salt to taste
½ tsp turmeric powder
2 tbsp lemon juice
1 tbsp coriander powder
¼ cup water
16 sweet peppers
¼ cup oil
¼ tsp mustard seeds

## Procedure

1. In a bowl add mashed potatoes, salt, turmeric powder, lemon juice, coriander powder and mix well.
2. Remove stems and peeps from all the peppers.
3. Fill the pepper with the stuffing.
4. In a pan heat oil, add mustard seeds and let them pop.
5. Add all the stuffed peppers gently in the pan and cook for 5 minutes stirring occasionally.

# Spicy Potatoes and Rice

## Ingredients

3 cups boiled rice
¼ cup oil
2 cups boiled and peeled potatoes
½ cup chopped onions
1 tsp turmeric powder
2 tsp coriander powder
2 tsp cumin powder
2 tbsp lemon juice

## Procedure

1. In a pan heat oil and add all the ingredients and mix with a spoon gently.
2. Cook for 5 to 7 minutes on medium heat stirring occasionally.

**Serves: 4**

# Potato Bhajis

## Ingredients

2 cups grated potatoes
1 cup gram flour
½ cup semolina
½ tsp turmeric powder
Salt to taste
½ tsp chili powder
1 tsp crushed ginger
½ cup chopped fresh coriander
Oil for frying

## Procedure

1. In a bowl mix potato, gram flour, semolina, turmeric powder, salt, chili powder, ginger and coriander to make batter.
2. In a pan heat oil and gently drop scoops of batter using a spoon or by hand.
3. Fry turning occasionally until they turn golden brown.

# Spicy Potatoes with Cheese

# Ingredients

2 cups boiled and peeled baby potatoes
½ cup oil
1 tsp freshly crushed garlic
½ tsp turmeric powder
½ tsp coriander powder
½ tsp chili powder
Salt to taste
2 tbsp gram flour
¼ cup grated mozzarella cheese

# Procedure

1. In a pan heat oil and add garlic, turmeric powder, coriander, powder, chili powder, salt and gram flour and mix well on medium heat.
2. Stir for 2-3 minutes and then add potatoes, mix well and cook for 5 minutes.
3. Transfer the potatoes on serving dish and sprinkle cheese evenly.

**Serves: 4**

# Stuffed Potato Pie

# Ingredients (for Crust)

2 cups all-purpose flour
1 tsp yeast
½ tsp salt
½ tsp sugar
1 cup water

## Procedure

1. Mix all ingredients in a bowl and leave aside for the dough to raise.

# Ingredients (for Stuffing)

3 medium boiled potatoes (mashed)
2 strips of chopped spring onions
1 tsp salt
1 tsp chili flakes
2 cups grated cheese
Oil for shallow frying
10-inch frying pan

## Procedure

1. In a bowl add potatoes, onions, salt, chili flakes and mix together.
2. With a rolling pin, roll the dough into a 14-inch diameter circle.
3. Spread 1 cup grated cheese (approx. 8-inch diameter) on the rolled dough.
4. Add layer of the mashed potatoes on top of the cheese layer and finally add the left over 1 cup cheese on the potato layer.
5. Lift the edges of the rolled dough and bring towards the center and close it.
6. Rolled the stuffed pie into a 10-inch diameter circle.
7. In a pan add 3 tbsp oil and heat. Gently lift the stuffed pie and place it into the pan.
8. Cook on medium heat, turning occasionally until golden brown.

**Serves 4**

# Potato and Banana Cheesecake

# Ingredients

½ cup boiled potatoes (mashed)
½ cup fresh cream
½ cup cream cheese
¾ cup icing sugar
1-2 drops of yellow food color
1 tsp banana extract
½ banana (sliced)
2 -3 tbsp caramel sauce
1 cup crumbs of cookies
1 tsp butter
2 cocktail glasses

# Procedure

1. In a bowl add crumbs of cookies, butter and microwave for 1 minute.
2. Divide the crumble into two and put them into the glasses gently pressing with a spoon.
3. In a bowl add mashed potatoes, fresh cream, cream cheese, icing sugar, food colour, banana extract and mix well with an electric mixer.
4. Pour the mixture equally into the pre-prepared glasses over the crumble layer and let it set in a fridge for 1 hour.
5. Add slices of banana for decoration and caramel sauce; dust icing sugar over it.

**Serves 2**

Printed in the United States
by Baker & Taylor Publisher Services